Friends of GSD 1b

A story about friendship & Glycogen Storage Disease 1b

Written by Margot LaFreniere
Illustrated by Kelsey Diaz

This book is dedicated with love to my daughter Sophie
and all other GSD 1b warriors.

First printing, 2024

Hi, I'm Molly and I was born
with a rare disease called
Glycogen Storage Disease
1b. Also called GSD 1b.

Hi, I'm Luca. I want
to hear all about it!

Rare means that not many people in the world have it.

Let's start in the belly, or actually my liver. The liver is an organ in the body that stores extra sugar and turns it into energy when the body needs it.

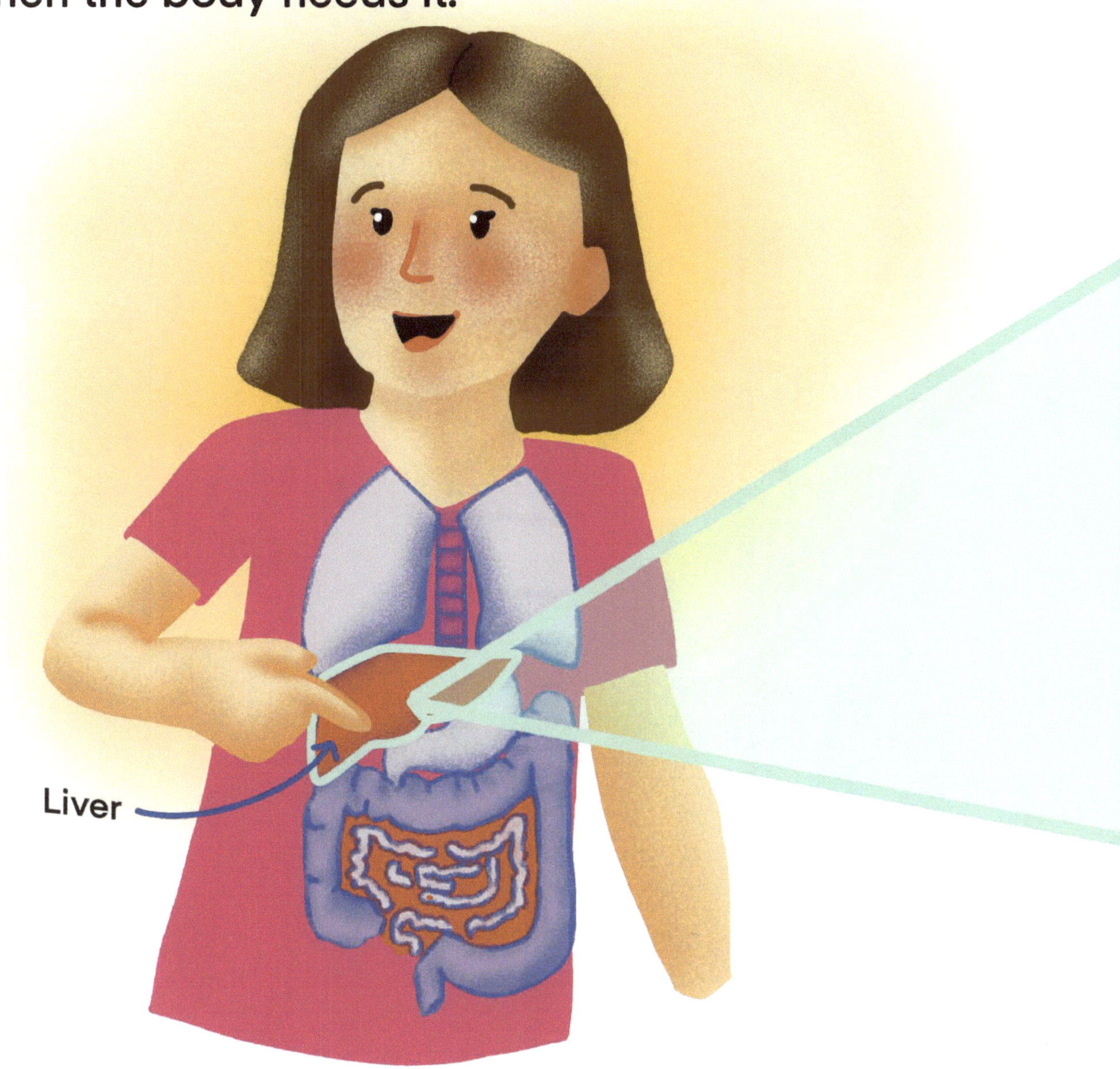

Because I have GSD, my liver can't do this.

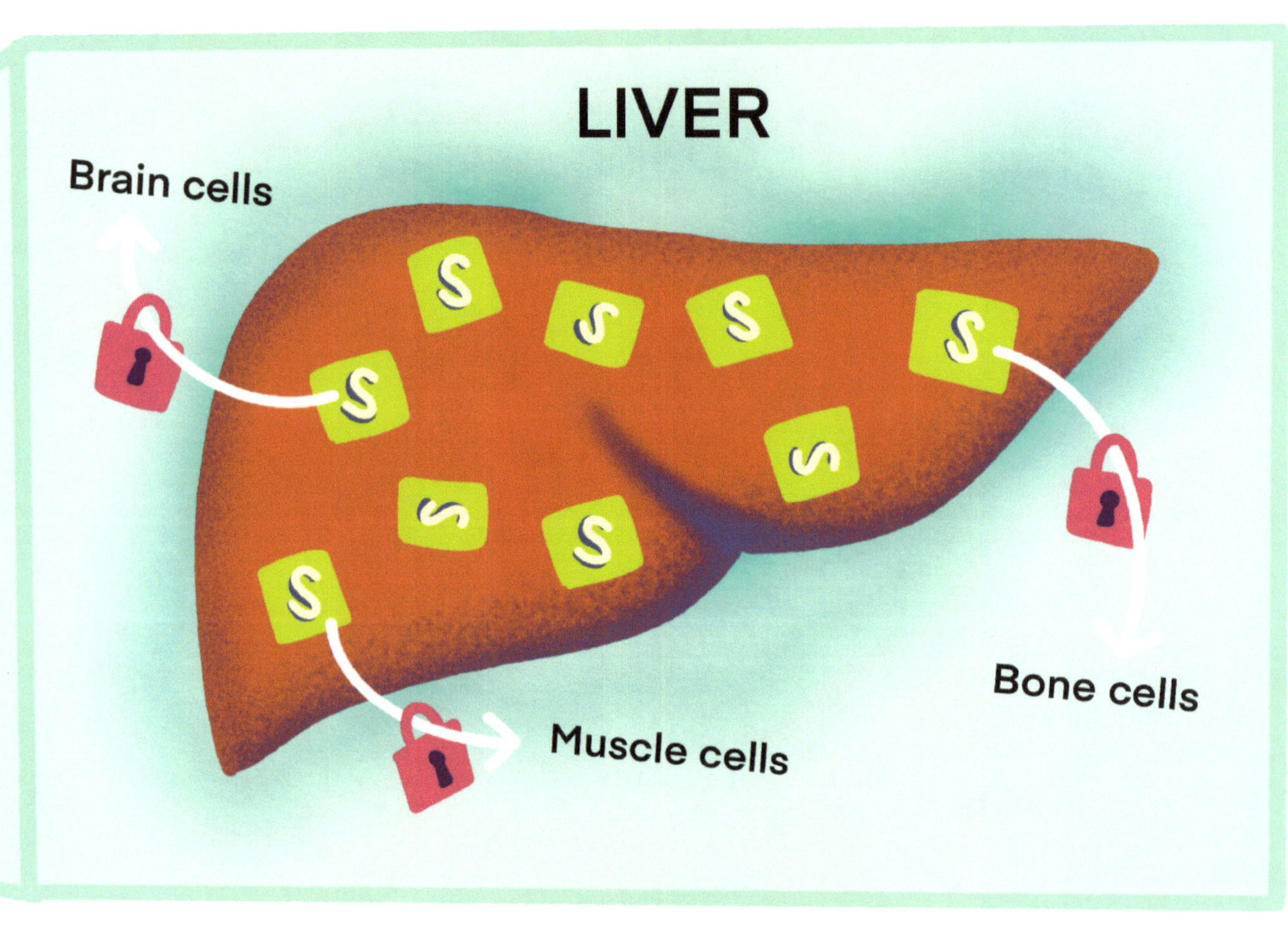

GSD stops my body from turning sugar into energy. So, I can have low blood sugars. Low blood sugars can make me feel bad. When my blood sugar is low, I feel weak, sweaty, dizzy, and tired.

That sounds yucky.
What do you do
when your blood
sugar is low?

It depends on how low
my blood sugar
number is. I will have a
snack or eat sugar gel.

Since my body works in a different way, I need
to do some things differently too. These things
keep my blood sugar up and keep me healthy.

I drink something
called cornstarch
many times a day to
keep my blood sugar
up. It is like my
medicine.

Wow!
How does
it work?

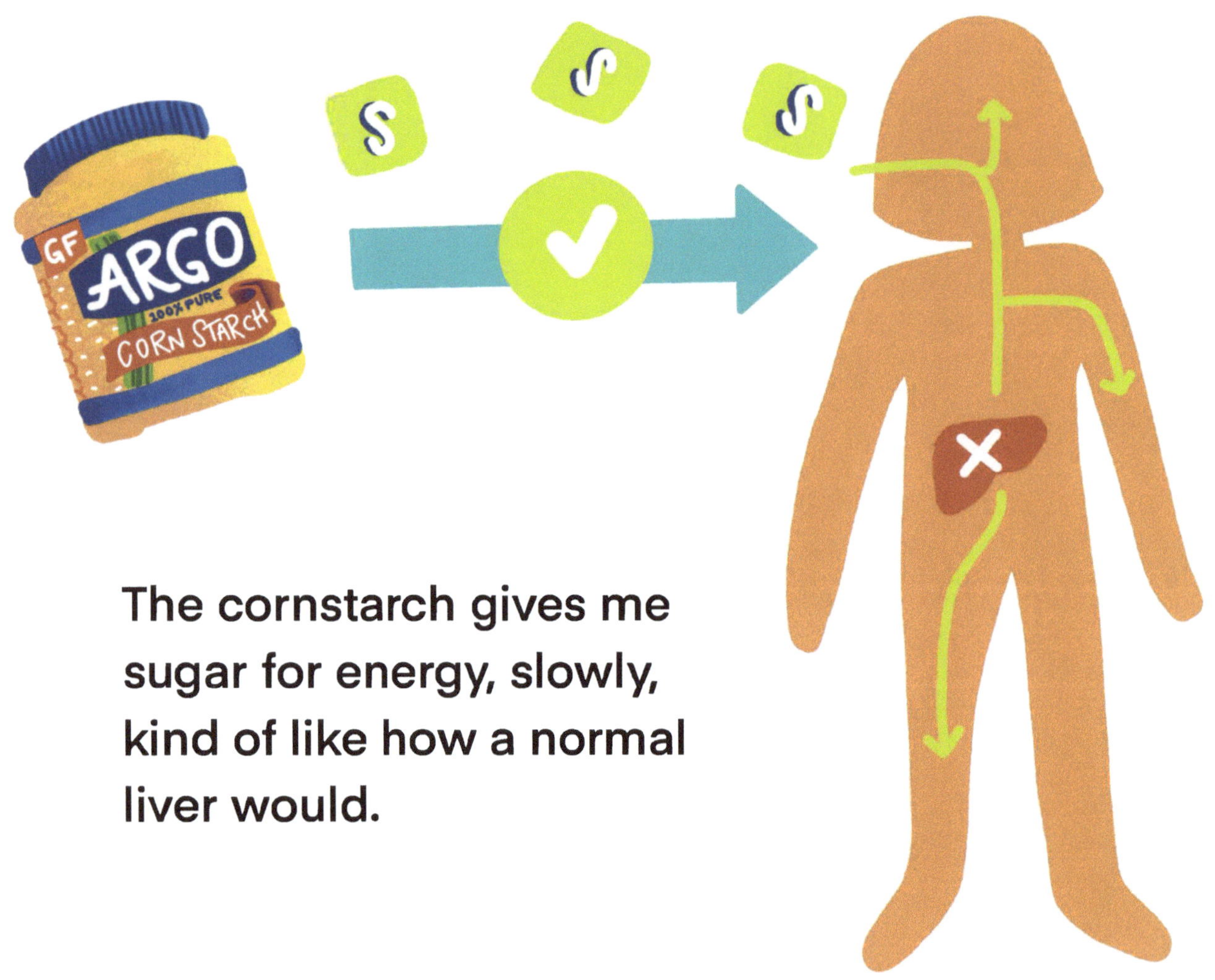

The cornstarch gives me sugar for energy, slowly, kind of like how a normal liver would.

Some people with GSD cannot drink their cornstarch so they use a feeding tube to get their cornstarch.

What is a feeding tube?

A feeding tube brings liquid food and medicines to the stomach without swallowing it.

What else do you have to do to keep yourself healthy with GSD?

Because my body can't use sugar and food in the same way as yours. I need to eat my meals at the same time each day and eat more often.

Oh, is there anything you can't eat?

Yes, because my body does not know what to do with extra sugar I can't eat much of it. That also means I do not eat much dairy and fruit.

Is that hard? Does that mean no ice cream? Or birthday cakes?

Yes. It stinks and sometimes it makes me feel left out. But, I can have sugar free candy and cakes! And, I try to make the best of it.

What's that patch on your arm?

This is my continuous glucose monitor.

What does that do?

It reads my blood sugar all the time. It sends my blood sugar number to my phone that I carry with me. This lets my parents and the school nurse know what my blood sugar number is all the time.

Sometimes it beeps loudly when my blood sugar level is low or if I get too far away from my phone. That can make me feel weird when everyone is looking at me wondering what the noise is.

Do you need to go
to the nurse a lot?

Yes, I do. I go there to have my finger pricked to test my blood sugar and drink my cornstarch a few times a day, but some people with GSD drink their cornstarch in the classroom.

Is there anything else you want me to know about you and GSD?

My body does not fight off germs like everyone else. So, I can get sick from germs.

That sounds hard. What can I do to help?

Wash your hands and stay home if you are sick.

Easy! I can do that!

Now that you have learned all about Glycogen Storage Disease 1b, you can help by teaching others about it too! Thank you for being a great GSD 1b friend!

To learn more about Glycogen Storage Disease type 1b or to help improve the lives of those affected by GSD 1b by making a donation please visit www.sophieshopefoundation.org.
If you would like more resources and educational material about GSD 1b please visit www.curegsd1b.org.